P9-DTW-522

ORIGINS

WHODUNNIT

Heists

C.M. Johnson

full tilt PRESS

Heists
Origins: Whodunnit

Full Tilt Press
42982 Osgood Road
Fremont, CA 94539
www.readfulltilt.com

Full Tilt Press publications may be purchased for educational, business, or sales promotional use.

Editorial Credits
Design and layout by Sara Radka
Edited by Lauren Dupuis-Perez
Copyedited by Renae Gilles

Image Credits
Getty Images: 5, 11, Chris Hondros, 7, EyeEm Premium, 37, Image Source, 28, iStockphoto, 4, 24, 29, 30, 34, 36, 41, Julien M. Hekimian, 21, Lawrence Lucier, 38, Matthew Peyton, 43, Rob Stothard, 32, Science Photo Library RF, 31; Newscom: Bizu/Splash News, 20, CSU Archives/ Everett Collection, 36, JT Vintage / Glasshouse Images, 40, ZUMAPRESS/Keystone Pictures USA, 26, ZUMAPRESS/NY Department of Correctional Se, 33, ZUMAPRESS/PA Wire, 10, 27, ZUMAPRESS/Paul Faith/PA Wire, 39; Shutterstock: Everett Historical, 13, 18, HUANG Zheng, 16, Wollertz, 6, Vecteezy: cover and background elements; Wikimedia: 14, 17, Barrow Gang, 9, Google Art Project, 15, 19, The Telegraph, 23, U.S. Army Corps of Engineers, 8

ISBN: 978-1-62920-615-8 (library binding)
ISBN: 978-1-62920-627-1 (eBook)

Printed in the United States of America.

Table of Contents

BANK HEISTS

Thieves looking to get a lot of cash sometimes break into locked rooms called vaults. Most of a bank's cash and other valuables are stored there.

Introduction

The word "heist" comes from "hoist," which means "to lift." Bank thieves hope to "lift" a pile of cash. Then they plan to slip away, never to be found.

In the movies, these heists are often clever. They are also complex. A team of experts join up to make it happen. A "mastermind" makes a plan. A locksmith **cracks** the safe. A fast driver speeds away in the getaway car. In real life, bank heists are often less organized. But some thieves are inspired by Hollywood's heists. In the 2010 movie *The Town*, four friends rob a string of banks. That same year, a group of men in New York carried out 62 real robberies. They poured bleach on ATMs to get rid of **DNA**. They used headlamps to see in the dark. When they were caught, they told police they got these tricks from the movie.

Bank robbers often wear masks to keep their hair and face hidden.

DID YOU KNOW?

In 1995, thieves imitating the movie *Money Train* set fire to a subway worker's booth. Unlike the character in the movie, who escaped, subway worker Harry Kaufman died from his burns.

crack: to open illegally without having a key or combination

DNA: the material in cells that provides the code for physical traits such as eye and skin color; this information can link people to crimes

The Biggest Heists

The world's biggest bank heist took place in Iraq. On March 18, 2003, at the start of the Iraq War (2003–2011), President Saddam Hussein sent his son and a close advisor with an order to the Central Bank. They took a lot of the country's money, an amount equal to $1 billion in US dollars. The bank did not dare defy the **dictator** president. So the biggest bank heist was probably also the easiest.

Instead of escaping Iraq with the money he stole, Saddam Hussein had to go into hiding. Eventually, US forces captured him.

In the second-biggest heist, thieves had to work harder. The theft was done by a fake landscaping company in the spring of 2005. The thieves set up a storefront in the city of Fortaleza, Brazil. Loads of dirt were trucked away each day. No one thought much of it. This was normal work for landscapers. Two blocks away was Banco Central. On Monday, August 8, the bank staff made a shocking discovery. The vaults were empty. Over the weekend, the vault had been blasted open. Behind the hole was a tunnel, 262 feet (80 meters) long. The tunnel led to the fake landscaping business. The thieves had spent three months digging it. They made off with $69.8 million.

dictator: a ruler with absolute power

Between 2005 and 2007, police got back about $20 million from the landscaping heist in Brazil. They believed that 25–40 thieves were involved. They arrested several of them. Many are still free. Others have been found dead. In October 2005, the mastermind of the plan, Luis Fernando Ribeiro, was kidnapped. In the crime world, it was known that Ribeiro had lots of money from the heist. His family paid $890,000 in **ransom**. The kidnappers killed him anyway.

ransom: the price demanded to be paid in exchange for the release of a prisoner

While stationed in Iraq, US soldiers found some of the money Saddam Hussein had stolen. Some soldiers tried to take more than $12 million for themselves, before getting caught by military officials.

History of Heists

Since banks have existed, bank heists have been a tempting crime.

1798

In the first US bank robbery, Isaac Davis and Thomas Cunningham make off with $162,821 from the Bank of Pennsylvania in Philadelphia.

1863

The first armed bank robbery in the United States takes place in Malden, Massachusetts. Edward Green shoots a 17-year-old clerk and steals $5,000. Green is caught when he starts paying off his debts.

1869

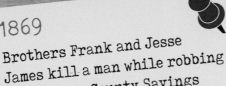

Brothers Frank and Jesse James kill a man while robbing the Daviess County Savings Association in Gallatin, Missouri. They steal only a stack of worthless bank papers that Jesse grabs as he runs away.

1932-1934

Bonnie Parker and Clyde Barrow commit at least 10 bank robberies, often stealing as little as $80 and killing many people.

1987

At the Knightsbridge Safe Deposit Centre in London, Valerio Viccei and fellow thieves tell bank employees that they want a safety deposit box. They hold the guards at gunpoint and take $49-73 million.

2016

John Walter Wilson demands a bag of cash at the Tri Counties Bank in McKinleyville, California. While trying to make his escape, he is chased down and held by a 58-year-old female citizen of the town.

While looking into the Knightsbridge Safe Deposit Centre robbery, London investigators found a fingerprint at the scene. This clue led them to Valerio Viccei. Viccei was already wanted for 50 robberies.

Catching a Thief

The Federal Deposit Insurance Corporation protects banks in the United States. It **insures** the money people deposit. The US government must refund stolen money. Other nations have similar systems. For this reason, officials take bank heists seriously. They want to find that cash. The **FBI** solves about 70 percent of US bank heists. They often give nicknames to thieves. The TV news is more likely to cover a colorful story. Viewers like to hear about the "Toothless Bandit" or the "Reckless Robber." The names are paired with pictures, as many thieves are caught on security cameras. Often, a TV viewer identifies the thief.

insure: to promise to pay for something if it is lost or damaged

FBI: Federal Bureau of Investigation, a national US security organization that investigates crimes and threats

DIRTY WORK

The FBI knew that Amil Dinsio was a bank robber. But they could not convict him. Dinsio never left evidence behind. In March 1972, Dinsio and his team robbed a bank in Laguna Niguel, California. They spent hours cleaning up. They wiped away every fingerprint and tire track. The FBI recognized Dinsio's work. Flight records showed Dinsio had flown to California from his home in Ohio under his own name. The FBI also found his California hideout. Like the bank's vault, the hideout

had been wiped clean—with one exception. The dishwasher had been loaded, but not run. It was filled with dirty dishes. The FBI found fingerprints, and Dinsio was sent to jail.

The FBI often focuses on big thefts. Thieves who take small amounts are more likely to escape. Carl Gugasian robbed at least 50 US banks before he was caught in 2002. For 30 years, he stayed free. Gugasian would enter a bank moments before it closed, when it was likely that no other customers would be there. He took only what he could grab from the **tills**.

In 1987, another thief named Valerio Viccei almost got away with his crime. He led a big heist in London. Then he fled to South America. He was free. But he decided to come back to England. His Ferrari, an expensive car, was there. He wanted to ship the car to his new home. While he was picking up the Ferrari, he was picked up by police.

till: a drawer for keeping money, especially in a place of business

Rooting for the Bad Guy

In the 1800s, "dime novels" were popular in the United States. These cheap books had lots of thrills. Many told stories about real-life outlaws. Jesse James was one of them. By 1903, James had shown up in 270 stories. In many of them, he is a hero. His thefts are full of drama. He seeks revenge when his friends are wronged. News editor John Newman Edwards also made James look heroic. In the 1870s, when James was active as a thief, Edwards wrote that James stole from the rich and gave to the poor. The public loved it. People began to cheer for James. Unfortunately, the claims were not true. James was not really so noble. He liked attention. He bragged about his crimes. He also shot **unarmed** bank clerks. He cracked their skulls with the butt of his pistol.

In the early 1900s, films were made about outlaws. The films made robbery look even more **glamorous**. The heists were exciting. The thieves were skilled. They were handsome and charming. Crime experts began to worry. They said people might be **corrupted** by the films. These experts told filmmakers to be more careful. They must not make crime look so smart and fun. But filmmakers said the crimes made great stories. With movies like *Money Train* and *The Town* inspiring modern criminals, this debate continues today.

> ### DID YOU KNOW?
> In the 1921 movie *Jesse James Under the Black Flag*, the character of Jesse James was played by his own son, Jesse Edwards James.

unarmed: not having a weapon

glamorous: to have a mysterious charm and style

corrupt: to become evil or dishonest

At the age of 16, Jesse James fought for the South in the American Civil War (1861–1865). After the war, he joined a gang of bank robbers and other outlaws.

ART HEISTS

More than 100 years ago, Leonardo da Vinci's *Mona Lisa* was at the center of an art theft mystery that took two years to solve.

Introduction

For a thief, stealing a painting has both **pros and cons**. On one hand, a painting has a good weight-to-value ratio. This is a comparison of how much an object weighs to how much it is worth. A famous painting weighs only a few pounds. However, it can sell for $100 million. In $100 bills, $100 million weighs 2,200 pounds (1,000 kilograms). Art thefts can also seem fancy. Thieves who steal art are taking objects of beauty. This can make them feel their crime is a work of art, too.

However, once a heist is complete, what is an art thief to do? Can the painting be turned into cash? The theft of a famous painting will be on the news. No museum will buy stolen art. Most collectors won't either. A thief must look for a customer who does not mind that the painting must be kept a secret.

Jacob de Gheyn III, a 1632 portrait by the Dutch painter Rembrandt van Rijn, has been stolen and found four times since 1966, more times than any other painting in the world.

DID YOU KNOW?

The most expensive painting ever sold is Paul Gauguin's 1892 *When Will You Marry?*, bought in 2015 for $300 million by a museum in the country of Qatar.

pros and cons: arguments both for and against a course of action

After the theft of the *Mona Lisa* from the Louvre was discovered, police searched for the painting in every wagon, car, truck, train, and boat leaving Paris.

The Biggest Heists

Museums are often closed on Mondays. This was the case on Monday, August 21, 1911, at the Musée du Louvre in Paris, France. On that day, the floors were cleaned. Paintings were taken down and repaired.

The Louvre had several paintings by the very famous painter Leonardo da Vinci. One was a small portrait called the *Mona Lisa*. On Tuesday, staff noticed that the *Mona Lisa* was gone. Vincenzo Peruggia, an Italian working and living in France, had taken it. He and two other thieves had come into the Louvre on Sunday. They hid in a storeroom. The next morning, they put on the outfits that museum employees wore. They came out and took the *Mona Lisa* down. No one took any notice. The men slipped out a side door, and Peruggia took the painting home.

The press went wild. Who could have done it? The poet Guillaume Apollinaire was accused. Then the artist Pablo Picasso. Both had been connected to a theft from the Louvre four years before. But this time, there was no evidence against them. They were let go. Meanwhile, Peruggia was thinking about the painting he had stashed in a wooden trunk. The *Mona Lisa* was Italian. It had been painted by the great Leonardo da Vinci. Peruggia could try to sell it in France. But did France really deserve it? Peruggia did not have good feelings about France.

In 1913, Peruggia wrote to an Italian gallery. He brought the *Mona Lisa* back to Italy. He tried to sell it for $100,000. The gallery owner promptly called the police, and Peruggia was arrested. The thief then told the press he had "rescued" the painting for Italy. The Italian public loved him. Their support swayed the judge, and Peruggia was released.

Vincenzo Peruggia had once worked for the Louvre. He was hired to build a protective glass case for the same painting he later stole.

History of Heists

When a famous work of art is stolen, the people behind the theft often become famous, too.

1940s

During World War II, Hitler and his top Nazi aides take paintings from conquered cities for their private collections.

1990

In the biggest art heist in US history, two men dress up as police officers, tie up the guards at the Boston, Massachusetts, Isabella Stewart Gardner Museum, and take 13 paintings worth a total of $300 million.

2000

At the National Museum in Stockholm, Sweden, paintings by Pierre-Auguste Renoir and Rembrandt van Rijn are stolen. Thieves set off car bombs on the other side of town to distract police, then escape in a speedboat.

2002

Thieves rent a store near the National Museum of Fine Arts in Asunción, Paraguay. They dig an 80-foot (24-meter) tunnel into the museum and steal more than $1 million in paintings.

2002

Octave Durham, known as the "Monkey," uses a ladder to climb up to a window of the Van Gogh Museum in Amsterdam, Netherlands. The paintings he steals are found 14 years later in Italy, in the house of a rich crime boss and drug dealer.

2004

Edvard Munch's famous painting *The Scream* is stolen when thieves hold guards at gunpoint at the Munch Museum in Oslo, Norway. It is recovered two years later.

2017

Yonathan Birn, on trial for the 2010 theft of five paintings from the Paris Museum of Modern Art, claims he threw the paintings in the garbage. The judge does not believe him.

The Isabella Stewart Gardner Museum in Boston is hoping the public can help them recover paintings stolen almost 30 years ago.

Catching a Thief

The biggest art heist in US history is unsolved. The paintings stolen from Boston's Isabella Stewart Gardner Museum in 1990 are still missing. Boston officials have said they will not charge the thieves. They just want the paintings back. The museum has also offered a $5 million reward to anyone who offers information that leads to the recovery of the works.

Some thieves are not caught, but their thefts are still not much of a success. In 1991, thieves broke into the Van Gogh Museum in Amsterdam. They forced guards to turn off the alarms. Then they looked at the museum's art for 45 minutes. Apparently, they were deciding what to take. They stole 20 paintings. Then, a half hour later, the works were found at a train station. Some of the art had been badly torn. The thieves had dumped the paintings. No one knew why.

MONUMENTS MEN

Wars are hard on art. Often, pieces are destroyed. Others are stolen by conquering armies. During World War II (1939–1945), the Nazi army took many paintings from museums and from Jewish families in Europe. In 1943, a group of 345 volunteers from 14 countries came together. These were the "Monuments Men." Their goal was to protect art and monuments located in the war zones. The group also tracked down stolen art, then gave it back to its rightful owners. After the war, the group put on exhibits and concerts. They helped bring war-torn Europe back to life through its art and music. In 2014, the movie *The Monuments Men* told their story.

In December 2005, a 2-ton (1.8-metric ton) sculpture was stolen in England. Thieves used a crane and a truck to haul it away. The piece was worth $4 million. But buyers must have been hard to find. The sculpture was melted down and sold as scrap metal. The thieves got only a few thousand dollars.

Rooting for the Bad Guy

Thefts can drive up the value of art. Before 1911, only a few art critics talked about the *Mona Lisa*. It was just a picture of a woman. Other works in the Louvre were more popular. The *Mona Lisa* did not get a lot of attention. Then it was stolen. Suddenly, the *Mona Lisa* was the most famous painting in the world.

> **DID YOU KNOW?**
>
> Vincenzo Peruggia thought the *Mona Lisa* had been stolen from Italy by the French emperor Napoleon Bonaparte. In fact, da Vinci brought the painting to France himself in 1516.

It is a big risk to take a painting. Why take such a chance? Why did Vincenzo Peruggia want it so badly? If he was willing to risk jail time, people thought, the *Mona Lisa* must be a big deal. People also liked Peruggia's story. He said he loved the painting. He wanted to give it back to Italy. He said he would have liked to have been an artist himself.

While it was still missing, long lines formed at the Louvre. Staff had never seen such lines. People were not there to see the paintings still hanging on the walls. They were more interested in the blank space the *Mona Lisa* had left behind. In the two days after it came back to France, 100,000 people came to see it. Today, the painting is valued at $1 billion.

In 1913, Giovanni Poggi was the director of the Uffizi Gallery in Florence, Italy. He was one of the men who turned Vincenzo Peruggia in to police when Peruggia tried to sell the *Mona Lisa*.

CASH & JEWEL HEISTS

Large amounts of cash are transported between places of business and banks every day. That much money on the move is a big temptation for thieves.

Introduction

Not every item of value is in a museum or a bank. Thieves study how cash and jewels are moved from place to place. It is hard to guard something when it is moving. Thieves look for weak spots in security, when **goods** are changing hands. In 1869, the new US rail system linked the East Coast to the West. Thieves like Jesse James took note. Rich people were on those trains. They carried cash. They wore diamond rings. Trains went through many rural spots. No law enforcement was nearby.

Today, thieves rob warehouses. These can hold valuable items waiting to be shipped. **Armored** cars are targeted for the cash they carry. Heists also occur in airports. Most of these places are guarded. Cash and jewel thieves must plan carefully. If a theft takes an unexpected turn, the thieves must also think on their feet.

DID YOU KNOW?

In Jesse James's first train robbery in 1873, he removed a rail from the track, sending a boiling-hot steam train crashing into a ditch. The crew was **scalded**, and the engineer was killed.

goods: personal property or merchandise that can be moved from one place to another

scalded: to be burned by hot liquid or steam

armored: covered with a tough protective material, often bulletproof

The Biggest Heists

On August 8, 1963, 15 British men pulled off the biggest cash heist in history. It was three o' clock in the morning. A mail train was heading from Glasgow to London. It was carrying a large amount of cash. About 30 miles (48 kilometers) from London, engineers saw a red signal. They slowed down. But they were puzzled. Why were they being delayed? Engineer David Whitby left the train to check. He found a glove covering the green signal. The red one was wired to a battery pack. It had been fixed to stop the train. Soon after his discovery, Whitby was attacked from behind. Masked men forced him back onto the train. They handcuffed him to the other engineer. The thieves then busted into a second train car. They overwhelmed the stunned mail clerks. They threw 120 sacks of cash down an **embankment**. Three vehicles were waiting, and the money was sped away. The train had been stopped for only 15 minutes. The thieves had made off with $7 million.

Most of the cash stolen from the 1963 mail train to London was made up of old paper bills that were going to be taken out of circulation and destroyed.

embankment: a raised structure built of earth or gravel, used to support a road or railway

The *New York Times* compared the theft to Jesse James's train heists. Some British journalists said the mail trains should have armed guards. The Postmaster General, the head of the British postal service, did not agree. He said, "The last thing we want is shooting matches on British railways."

Local police spent the day of the 1963 mail train robbery searching nearby homes, but they found nothing.

History of Heists

Cash and jewels may be hard to trace, but heists leave their mark in time.

1983

A bribed security guard lets six men into a Brink's-Mat warehouse in London. They steal $32 million in gold and jewels.

1978

Mobster Jimmy Burke organizes the biggest cash heist ever in the United States. His team steals about $6 million in cash and jewelry from Lufthansa Airlines at John F. Kennedy International Airport in New York.

1994

Robbers walk into the jewelry shop of the Carlton Hotel in Cannes, France, firing off machine guns. They escape with $45 million in jewels. Later, police see there are no bullet holes in the walls. The thieves were firing blanks.

2003

The School of Turin is a group of Italian thieves who never use violence. In one of their biggest heists, they pose as diamond merchants. They steal $100 million in jewels from the Antwerp World Diamond Centre in Belgium. The ringleader is caught when evidence is lifted from half a sandwich that he left behind.

2008-2009

In California, a gang of Hollywood teenagers known as the "Bling Ring" steal $3 million in jewelry and clothing from the homes of stars such as Paris Hilton and Orlando Bloom.

2016

In Maryland, a guard moving cash from an armored truck into a SunTrust Bank is robbed by two men carrying assault rifles.

Diamonds are one of the most popular gemstones. They are the most common gem found in engagement rings.

Catching a Thief

Jewel heists often go well. Gems are easy to hide. It is also hard to spot stolen diamonds. They are easier to sell than art, when the whole world knows a particular painting has been stolen. Lazare Kaplan International is a company that turns rough diamonds into shiny jewels. They have created a way to identify gems. A laser cuts a tiny mark on the gem that an expert can spot. Of course, a dishonest expert can also cut off the mark. In 1994, the Cannes jewel thieves got away with their crime. Police got back some of the goods from the Brink's-Mat heist. However, the thieves melted down some of the gold. They sold it, and used the money to buy land and drugs. Only two of the thieves went to jail.

Cash is harder to use once it has been stolen. Bills can be marked. They can be traced by their **serial numbers**. After the 1963 British train robbery, a local man led police to the thieves' hideout. There, they found fingerprints on a Monopoly game. The thieves had used the stolen money to play it. The 15 thieves were arrested, though their "inside man" in the postal service was never caught. Police also found 10 percent of the cash. If any was left by 1971, it did not matter. In that year, Great Britain changed its **currency**. Most of the stolen cash could no longer be used.

serial number: a number printed or stamped on an object to identify it and to indicate the order in which it was made

currency: the type of paper money or coins being used in a particular country

CHRISTMAS SURPRISE

In November 1983, the thieves in the Brink's-Mat heist knew there were 3 million pounds ($3.7 million) in the vault. Their inside man had told them so. The 7,000 gold bars, however, were a surprise. The unexpected gift put them in a holiday mood. As they were leaving, one of the thieves wished a merry Christmas to the security guards they had tied up and covered with gasoline. Thankfully, the guards were not harmed.

In 2014, a model railway set showing the Great Train Robbery of 1963 was put on display at the London Festival of Railway Modeling.

Rooting for the Bad Guy

In 1964, 12 of the British train robbers who had pulled off the biggest cash heist in history went on trial. A judge told the jury to ignore the newspapers. This was because the thieves had gotten a lot of good press. England was in an economic **slump**, and many people were poor. People were delighted by the heist. They admired the planning that went into it. Also, the thieves seemed like ordinary guys. They were struggling like most of the country. One thief was a florist. Another sold old furniture. The crime let people dream. What would they do with $7 million? The judge gave the thieves harsh sentences. He did not want to encourage people toward a life of crime.

slump: a decline in activity or prices

In the United States, the press loved the 1978 Lufthansa heist. It was a complex crime. Mastermind Jimmy Burke had to get permission from several Mafia families to pull it off. Unfortunately, the heist led to a lot of bloodshed. After the theft, Burke began to get angry. His fellow thieves were not following orders. He had told them to lay low. Instead, they bought fur coats and fancy cars with the stolen money. Burke ended up killing at least 10 of his fellow thieves. The story was turned into the 1990 movie *Goodfellas*. It became one of the most famous movies of all time.

James Burke, known as "Jimmy the Gent," was never convicted for the Lufthansa heist. He did spend many years in jail for other crimes, including murder, before his death in 1996.

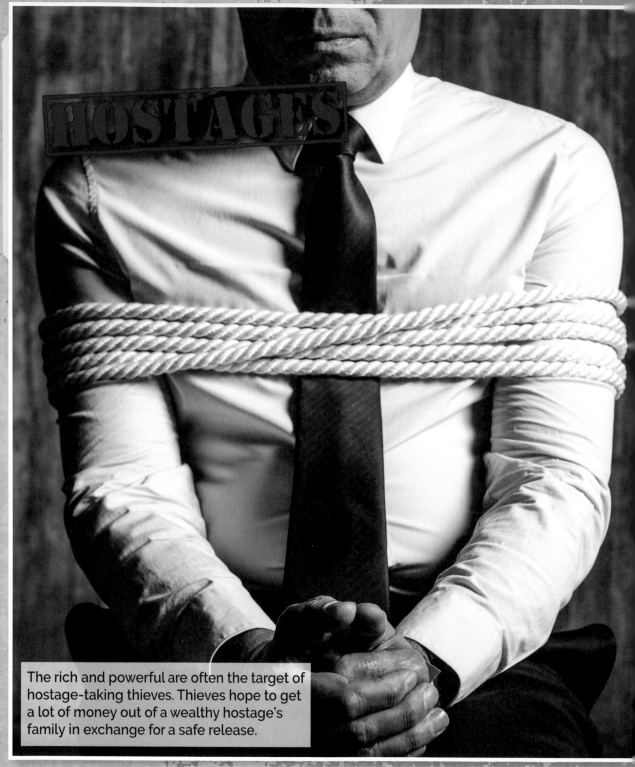

HOSTAGES

The rich and powerful are often the target of hostage-taking thieves. Thieves hope to get a lot of money out of a wealthy hostage's family in exchange for a safe release.

Introduction

A hostage is a prisoner. Criminals sometimes kidnap people during a heist. Instead of keeping this crime a secret, thieves let the police know they have hostages. They then use the hostages to **bargain**. At times, a hostage situation happens in a heist gone wrong. This is often the case in the movies. Thieves want to rob a bank at night, when no one is there. But it takes too long to open the vault. An employee shows up in the early morning. Now the employee has seen their faces. The thieves don't want to kill him, but they can't let him go. The thieves decide to make their prisoner useful.

In real heists, thieves often seek hostages. Then they refuse to let them go until a ransom is paid. The thieves might demand a sack of cash. They also use the hostages to escape. They might ask for a jet or a boat. In return, they promise to let the hostages go unharmed. They want to speed off unfollowed and start enjoying their money.

In hostage situations, police must talk with thieves about their demands, in order to keep the hostages safe.

DID YOU KNOW?

In ancient Egypt, military leaders often kidnapped the children of kings in the countries that they conquered. This way, the kings would not fight their new Egyptian leaders.

bargain: to argue about the terms or price of an agreement or sale

Investigators think that Dan Cooper might have worked at the Boeing Company, which made the Boeing 727 that Cooper hijacked.

The Biggest Heists

On November 24, 1971, the short Northwest Airlines flight from Portland, Oregon, to Seattle, Washington, was going smoothly. Then a passenger signaled the flight attendant. He was polite. He wore a suit and tie. The flight attendant thought that he probably only wanted another drink. He gave her a note instead. It said he had a bomb. The man, who had checked in under the name Dan Cooper, showed the flight attendant a briefcase filled with wires. Then he made his demands. He wanted four parachutes and $200,000. If he did not get it, he would blow up the plane.

After the hijacking, a police sketch artist used descriptions of Dan Cooper by crew members and passengers to draw a picture of the thief.

In Seattle, Cooper was given what he wanted. He let the 36 passengers go. But his heist was not over. He kept the pilot and part of the crew. He told the pilot to set a **course** for Mexico City, Mexico. He said the pilot must fly as low and slowly as possible. Cooper ordered the crew to stay in the cockpit with the pilots. He put on a parachute. At around 8 p.m., he opened the rear door of the plane. Then he jumped out with his cash and was never seen again.

course: a route or plan for how to get from one place to another

Could Dan Cooper have survived a parachute jump into a wild wooded area, in the dark of the night?

History of Heists

Taking hostages is risky and dangerous, yet some desperate thieves do it anyway.

1972

After watching the gangster movie *The Godfather* for inspiration, John Wojtowicz tries to rob a Chase Manhattan Bank in Brooklyn, New York. Police surround the bank before he can get out. Wojtowicz takes the bank employees hostage in exchange for escape, but is caught after 14 hours.

1974

Patty Hearst, granddaughter of the wealthy William Randolph Hearst, is kidnapped from her home in Berkeley, California. Her captors call themselves the Symbionese Liberation Army (SLA). They demand millions of dollars in food donations in exchange for Hearst's release.

1975

The film Dog Day Afternoon, based on the story of John Wojtowicz, is released by Warner Bros.

2004

In Belfast, Northern Ireland, masked men raid the homes of two bank executives and hold their families hostage. When the bank closes the next evening, the two executives lead the crooks into the vaults, where they steal $32.4 million before escaping.

2012

After a failed attempt to rob a jewelry factory, Brazilian thieves take nine hostages, including one child, into the woods around the city of Cotiporã. The hostages are rescued by police.

2016

At a McDonald's near Tampa, Florida, car thieves briefly hold the staff of the restaurant hostage after crashing their stolen car nearby.

Catching a Thief

John Wojtowicz's 1972 Brooklyn robbery did not go as planned. In fact, he and the friends he hired to help him tried to rob three other banks earlier that day, before they ended up at Chase Manhattan. At the first bank, one of them dropped his gun on the street. The gun went off and drew a crowd. The thieves had to run. At a bank in Queens, New York, they ran into a friend of one of their mothers. Again, they fled the scene. When they finally got into Chase Manhattan, the safe was only half-full. A staff member alerted the police, and the thieves could not get away in time. Soon, they were surrounded. They took the eight staff members hostage. After a 14-hour standoff, they were driven to the airport with their hostages. But once there, one of the robbers got into a struggle with an FBI agent over a gun, and was shot dead. The hostages were released unharmed and Wojtowicz was arrested. He went to jail for five years. After getting out, he struggled to make a living. He even applied unsuccessfully for a job as a security guard at the same bank he had tried to rob.

Dog Day Afternoon

John Wojtowicz was paid $100,000 for the film rights to the story of his 1972 bank robbery. His right to keep the money was fought in court. The New York State Crime Victims Compensation Board gave much of it to his hostages. Police do not want thieves to profit from their crimes. Other would-be criminals might try to do the same. Many states have passed laws to prevent **lucrative** deals for criminals.

Eight-year-old Brian Ingram was near Vancouver, Washington, clearing a spot for a camp fire, when he happened to dig up some of Dan Cooper's ransom money.

In 1971, police **combed** the deep forests where Dan Cooper had jumped from the plane. Many think he could not have survived. It was cold out on the night Cooper jumped. He was not wearing warm clothes. In 1980, a boy found a bag of $20 bills in the woods. They matched the serial numbers of Cooper's stolen money. Perhaps Cooper died in the fall. Why else would he have left $5,800 behind? Or did he leave it to throw police off track? No trace of his body was ever found.

lucrative: something that makes a lot of money

comb: to search carefully and thoroughly

Rooting for the Bad Guy

Hostage-takers use fear to get what they want. They want to show police that they are serious. Hostages do not know if they will live or die. Hostage-takers can be unpredictable. If things don't go according to plan, they sometimes just start killing people. In 1998, thieves tried to rob Ly Tai Jewelry in Fresno, California. They took the two owners hostage. The police forced their way into the shop. There, they found three bodies. The thieves had killed themselves. They had also killed one of their hostages. It was not clear why.

> ## DID YOU KNOW?
> Patty Hearst may have suffered from Stockholm syndrome. This is a mental condition in which hostages develop feelings of sympathy for their captors.

Some thieves convince hostages that their cause is **just**. The SLA told their hostage Patty Hearst that they were fighting to overthrow the government. They also said that rich people like her grandfather were evil. They said they wanted to rob banks to punish rich people. Hearst came to feel they were on the right side. She helped them rob banks. On September 18, 1975, the FBI caught Hearst. Her lawyer said she had been **brainwashed**, and that she wasn't responsible for her crimes. However, a jury found her guilty.

John Wojtowicz's robbery drew a huge audience. People outside the bank were soon cheering for him. He said he was fighting for the little guy. It did not hurt his case that he threw some of the bank's money to the crowd.

just: morally right or fair

brainwash: to force someone to make a huge change in their beliefs, often by using constant social pressure

Patty Hearst served almost two years in jail for taking part in the robbery of the Hibernia Bank in San Francisco with members of the SLA.

Most thieves don't get away with their crimes. They end up behind bars.

Conclusion

Is it true that "crime doesn't pay?" Some thieves profit from their crimes. Whoever stole paintings from the Isabella Stewart Gardner Museum never had to give them back. This heist was a success for the criminals, and no one was killed. For the rest of their lives, some thieves can think back on the day they outsmarted the police.

But do thieves ever get everything they want? They do not get to publicly tell their stories. They can't say, "It was me!" They can't brag about "how they did it." Thieves love to tell about their heists as much as we like to hear about them. This fact has led to the downfall of some criminals. They can't help themselves. They tell their secret to someone. Then that person goes to the police. Maybe the payoff of telling the story is as big a temptation as the money itself.

Glossary

armored: covered with a tough protective material, often bulletproof

bargain: to argue about the terms or price of an agreement or sale

brainwash: to force someone to make a huge change in their beliefs, often by using constant social pressure

comb: to search carefully and thoroughly

corrupt: to become evil or dishonest

course: a route or plan for how to get from one place to another

crack: to open illegally without having a key or combination

currency: the type of paper money or coins being used in a particular country

dictator: a ruler with absolute power

DNA: the material in cells that provides the code for physical traits such as eye and skin color; this information can link people to crimes

embankment: a raised structure built of earth or gravel, used to support a road or railway

FBI: Federal Bureau of Investigation, a national US security organization that investigates crimes and threats

glamorous: to have a mysterious charm and style

goods: personal property or merchandise that can be moved from one place to another

insure: to promise to pay for something if it is lost or damaged

just: morally right or fair

lucrative: something that makes a lot of money

pros and cons: arguments both for and against a course of action

ransom: the price demanded to be paid in exchange for the release of a prisoner

scalded: to be burned by hot liquid or steam

serial number: a number printed or stamped on an object to identify it and to indicate the order in which it was made

slump: a decline in activity or prices

till: a drawer for keeping money, especially in a place of business

unarmed: not having a weapon

Quiz

1 Where did the world's biggest bank heist take place?

2 How much money was stolen during the first bank robbery in the United States?

3 Who stole the *Mona Lisa* in 1911?

4 What was the name of Edward Munch's famous painting that was stolen in 2004?

5 Where did the biggest art heist in US history take place?

6 How much money did Jimmy Burke steal in 1978?

7 How much money did Dan Cooper demand?

8 What was the name of the group Patty Hearst was kidnapped by?

1. Iraq

2. $162,821

3. Vincenzo Peruggia

4. *The Scream*

5. Boston's Isabella Stewart Gardner Museum

6. About $6 million

7. $200,000

8. Symbionese Liberation Army

Index

Selected Bibliography

Amore, Anthony M. and Tom Mashberg. *Stealing Rembrandts: The Untold Stories of Notorious Art Heists.* New York: Palgrave Macmillan, 2011.

Patterson, Richard. *Train Robbery: The Birth, Flowering, and Decline of a Notorious Western Enterprise.* Boulder, Colo.: Johnson Books, 1981.

Rehder, William J. and Gordon Dillow. *Where the Money Is: True Tales from the Bank Robbery Capital of the World.* New York: W.W. Norton & Company, 2003.

Schroeder, Andreas. *Thieves! True Stories from the Edge.* Toronto: Annick Press, 2005.

"Jesse James and Frank James." *Encyclopædia Britannica Online.* Encyclopædia Britannica, n.d. Web. Accessed February 6, 2017. https://www.britannica.com/biography/Jesse-James-and-Frank-James/.

Zug, James. "Stolen: How the Mona Lisa Became the World's Most Famous Painting." *Smithsonian.com.* Smithsonian Institution, June 15, 2011. Web. Accessed February 6, 2017. http://www.smithsonianmag.com/arts-culture/stolen-how-the-mona-lisa-+became-the-worlds-most-famous-painting-16406234/.

Smith, Roff. "A Recent History of Diamond Heists." *National Geographic News.* National Geographic Partners, LLC, May 10, 2013. Web. Accessed February 6, 2017. http://news.nationalgeographic.com/news/2013/13/130509-diamond-heist-crime-jewel-thief/.

U.S. Department of Justice. "Patty Hearst." Washington, D.C.: Federal Bureau of Investigation, n.d. Web. Accessed February 6, 2017. https://www.fbi.gov/history/famous-cases/patty-hearst.